P9-EDY-860

ULTIMATE THRILL SPORTS

SNOWBOARDING

By Matt Barr

Gareth Stevens
Publishing

Please visit our web site at www.garethstevens.com
For a free catalog describing our list of high-quality books, call 1-800-542-2595 (USA) or
1-800-387-3178 (Canada). Our fax: 1-877-542-2596

ISBN-10: 0-8368-8963-0   ISBN-13: 978-0-8368-8963-5 (lib. binding)

ticktock project editor: Julia Adams
ticktock project designer: Sara Greasley
ticktock picture researcher: Lizzie Knowles

Gareth Stevens Senior Managing Editor: Lisa M. Guidone
Gareth Stevens Creative Director: Lisa Donovan
Gareth Stevens Art Director: Giovanni Cipolla
Gareth Stevens Associate Editor: Amanda Hudson

Picture credits (t=top; b=bottom; c=center; l=left; r=right):
ACM Group: 4/5, 9cl, 22/23t, 22cr, 31cl, 33b, 34b, 35bl, 54. AFP/Getty Images: 48/49. A Snowboards: 11t.
Abelboden Tourism: 7t. Matt Barr: 1, 61b. Mike Basich: 56. Blickwinkel/Alamy: 57b. Blotto/ Burton Snowboards: 6t,
8/9t, 23b, 43t, 51b, 55tl, 55tr. Breckenridge: 40. Burton Snowboards: 8b, 9b, 11c, 17 all, 18b, 20b, 21t, 21c, 29t,
35t, 35bc, 35br, 58t, 59c, 59b. Rita Cami: 28. Canadian Press/ Rex Features: 50. Jess Curtes/ Burton Snowboards:
59t, 61t. Dakine: 18c inset. Nick Hamilton: 30t. Martin Harvey/Corbis: 33t. Jackson Hole Mountain Resort: 26.
Jupier Images/Image Source Black: 22bl. Lech Tourism: 31t. Eddie Lee/thirtytwo snowboards: 47b. James McPhail:
13b, 14/15, 16, 18t, 18c, 20/21 main, 27b, 29b, 32, 38/39, 41b, 42, 44, 45b, 46b, 57c. Chris Moran: 45t, 58c.
Silvretta Nova: 46/47t. Oakley: 21b, 55. Ortovox: 37t. Damien Poullenot: 57t. Shutterstock: 2, 3, 12, 19, 24/25,
33b, 34t, 36. Sipa Press/ Rex Features: 52/53t, 52b, 53b. Squaw: 13t. Solomon Snowboards: 60.
STL/ICON/Actionplus: 51b. Ticktock Media Archive: 37b, 41t. Treble Cone: 7b. www.explore.co.uk: 57c.

Contents

chapter 1: introduction

Pro rider Chris Moran pushes snowboarding to a new level. He seeks out the impressive slopes in East Greenland, where temperatures can be as low as -85° Fahrenheit (-65° Celsius)!

Snowboarding is one of the world's most popular young sports. It attracts more people every year. Snowboarding means traveling, experiencing the outdoors, and having a fun, healthful time with your friends.

It's no wonder so many people are taking up this exciting sport. Fun and totally addictive, snowboarding offers endless opportunities for self-expression. It also gives people the chance to explore one of the most beautiful and adventurous environments on the planet: the mountains. Like its close cousins skateboarding and surfing, snowboarding is popular for many reasons, but many people enjoy it because it gives them a sense of freedom.

In this book, we will introduce you to the exciting world of shredding, or snowboarding. You'll learn how it all started and see some of the amazing mountains that are home to snowboarders. We will also explain snowboarding-speak and find out just what a "Roast Beef" trick is!

SNOWBOARDING

Snowboarders hit the slopes at Lake Louise Mountain Resort in Canada.

For most people, snowboarding means traveling to the mountains to get to the snow. It can be a great way to explore the world.

If you decide you want to master the board yourself, the best way is to get out there and start riding!

To get started, take a few lessons with a qualified instructor at your nearest slope.

Nobody really knows when the first snowboarder took that all-important sideways step. We do know that in 1914, Toni Lenhardt invented the mono-glider, an early snowboard. He was followed in 1939 by Vern Wicklund, who filmed himself riding on an early version. Look at these old boards to get an idea of the type of equipment snowboarders were riding back then.

These pioneers invented variations of the snowboard in the early twentieth century. But it wasn't until an American named Sherman Poppen invented a stand-up sled for his daughter in the 1960s that the sport really took off. It didn't sell very well, but it did inspire a generation of young skateboarders and surfers to design their own boards.

With no bindings to attach the rider's boots to the board, some of the first snowboards were a tricky ride!

Snowboarding became skiing's cooler younger brother.

The first commercial snowboard – "The Snurfer" by Brunswick Manufacturing – was released in 1965. It was meant to be a child's toy, but it was followed by a second wave of adult boards manufactured by surfer Dimitrije Milovich, who started Winterstick Snowboards in 1972.

Two snowboarding pioneers in the 1970s were Tom Sims and Jake Burton Carpenter. They created the Sims and Burton companies and started to grow the sport's popularity in the United States.

Tom Sims (far right) and Jake Burton Carpenter (far left) before one of the first snowboarding races (1983)

The monoski, an invention of the 1960s, consists of one ski. Unlike a snowboard, the rider faces forward.

By 1984, snowboarding was also becoming popular in Europe, thanks to Régis Rolland. Régis was a ski instructor from France who made Europe's first snowboarding film, *Apocalypse Snow*. The film was made in the winter of 1983 and released around the world. It helped bring the sport to another level of popularity outside the United States. In Europe, the monoski – a popular variation on "classic" skis involving just one ski – was still rising in popularity. In the next few years, it started giving way to the snowboard.

By the early 1990s, the world knew about snowboarding. Winter sports enthusiasts wanted a piece of the action. The sport doubled in size nearly every year. People like Jake Burton Carpenter, who started constructing snowboards in a barn in Vermont in 1977, suddenly found their businesses expanding to meet the demands of the world's snowboarders.

A scene from *Apocalypse Snow*

Classic Films

Régis Rolland made three
Apocalypse Snow films.
Régis was introduced to
snowboarding in 1981,
when a couple of American
pro riders visited France
and gave him a board.
He began to film his friends
riding and ended up making
this legendary series. The
films feature some incredible
footage and are a great
example of how exciting
snowboarding can be. They
are considered classic
snowboarding films by
many of today's riders.

Jake Burton Carpenter constructs
an early snowboard.

Today, snowboarding is the world's
most popular winter sport. There are an
estimated eight to fourteen million
snowboarders. That number continues
to grow.

As the sport of snowboarding evolved, many different styles developed. Today it's possible to be a "freerider," a "freestyler," and even a "jibber"! Confused? Let us explain.

Freeriding

Most snowboarders stick to marked trails (known as "pistes" in Europe) when they are on the mountain. But freeriding is the art of using the whole mountain as a playground. Freeriders like to ride in deep powder snow, find the steepest parts of the mountain, and even jump off cliffs! It can be thrilling and extremely dangerous.

A half pipe gets its name from the shape – it is literally half a pipe!

Freestyle

In freestyle, snowboarders take the tricks of skateboarding and surfing and perform them on snow. Resorts build big snow jumps and obstacles so that freestylers can perform their tricks. Half pipes are especially popular.

Jibbing

Jibbing is a great example of how snowboarding constantly evolves as people learn new things. Jibbing has its roots in skateboarding, where people ride objects such as handrails and concrete ledges on their boards. Snowboarders quickly copied skateboarding. An entirely new kind of snowboarder was born. Today, jibbing is popular among young riders.

13

chapter 2: gear and fashion

There may be a standard set of gear for snowboarding, but who's to say you can't have your own individual style?

Without snow, there would be no snowboarding. But this means that riders need to protect themselves from the weather conditions found in the mountains. Riders also need proper gear to handle the different types of snow.

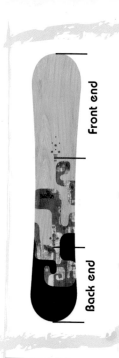

Front end

Back end

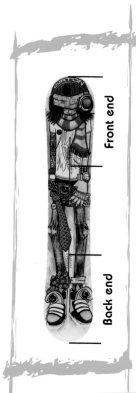

Front end

Back end

Front end

Back end

Freeride Board

When most people think of snowboarding, they probably think of freeriding – long slopes and lots of snow. Freeride boards are wider so they can "float" better on top of deep snow. They are long, too, so they can go faster. The board tends to be longer at the front than at the back, so the rider is able to "surf" the snow.

Freestyle Board

Freestyle is all about performing spectacular tricks, which means a freestyle board needs to enable the rider to jump and spin with ease. Freestyle boards tend to be shorter and have a nose and tail that are the same length, so the rider can move backward and forward. They are also lighter.

Powder Board

When pro riders go into extreme conditions, sometimes they take a special powder board. Powder boards are very long. They are designed to be ridden as quickly as possible, on steep slopes with deep snow. If the board has a shorter or lighter tail, the rider's weight is at the back of the board. This makes the board glide better on the snow. One type of powder board is called "The Fish" because it floats so well!

17

E ven though there are many different types of board, they all have the same basic elements. These are the most important features:

Deck and Base

Deck   Base

The upper surface of the snowboard is called the deck. The rider's feet strap to this surface. The part that is in contact with the snow is called the base. Riders put wax on the base of their boards to make sure they slide well.

Metal Edges

Snow can be icy, soft, or slushy, so it is very important for a board to have sharp metal edges. They help the board turn by cutting into the snow. Early snowboards didn't have metal edges, which made it difficult to get the board to grip on snow and ice.

Bindings

Bindings attach the rider to the board by his or her feet. They are usually made out of plastic and metal and clamp the feet into place securely.

Metal edges were first used on the Sims 1500FE and the Burton Performer snowboards in 1985. Until then, ice was much more of a challenge!

Being exposed to the elements means that snowboarders have to wear the right clothing. The right gear protects snowboarders from the sun and snow. It also keeps them safe when they fall.

A snowboarder in typical gear

Boots:

Snowboard boots are designed to fit the bindings of the board and keep the rider securely attached to it. They also offer support and protection.

Gloves:

Gloves are essential, because snowboarders spend most of the day with their hands in the snow. Snow gloves are hard-wearing, waterproof, and warm inside.

Helmet:

Smart riders wear a helmet when they snowboard. Hidden rocks can be dangerous, especially for freeriders. Plenty of riders have also landed on their heads while performing tricks in fun parks.

Goggles:

Goggles protect the rider's eyes from spraying snow when he or she is going down a slope. They also guard eyes from the sun and from the danger of snow blindness.

Snow blindness Snow blindness can happen when sunlight reflects off the snow. The ultraviolet rays in the reflected sunlight can cause an effect similar to a sunburn on the eye. Symptoms can run from bloodshot and teary eyes to permanent vision loss.

Although it is important for clothing to protect the rider, it can still be fashionable. Like skateboarding, fashion has always had an important role in the sport.

The 1980s – The Neon Years

In the 1980s, snowboarders were influenced by the bright neon colors of the surf world.
As you can see in the picture to the right, that meant lots of bright yellows, reds, and patterns.

The 1990s – The Baggy Revolution

By the 1990s, the surf influence was being left behind. Skateboarding and hip hop influences became more important. Riders began to wear baggy clothes in muted colors and to sport dreadlocks.

Today – Fashion and Function

Snowboarding is still a highly fashion-conscious sport. Many riders like to make sure that the clothes they wear express their individual tastes, along with keeping them warm and dry. Clothing brands now make high-quality gear that is more visually striking every year.

chapter 3:the mountain

With peaks of up to 15,774 feet (4,808 meters) and snowfall all year round, the Alps in Europe are one of the most popular winter sport destinations in the world.

There are many amazing mountains in the world. Snowboarders have many choices. Some of the world's best resorts offer towering peaks, blindingly fast runs, and huge jumps. Here are a few of the places where snowboarders can get their kicks.

A resort in Breckenridge, Colorado

Colorado

The United States is the home of snowboarding. It has some of the world's best riders and the biggest resorts, many of them in Colorado and other Rocky Mountain states. Riders seeking the best pipes and trickiest jumps will come here to seek thrills and catch big air.

Alps

The Alps, which cover parts of several countries (including France, Switzerland, Austria, and Italy), have long been known for their beautiful and challenging resorts. They are popular with snowboarders all over the world. The Alpine slopes are especially popular among snowboarders. The world speed snowboarding record was set in the Alps. Riders with the need for speed seek out these incredibly steep runs.

A slope signpost at the Méribel resort in the French Alps

Mount Tasman, New Zealand

New Zealand

New Zealand has incredible conditions to offer riders when it is summer in the Northern Hemisphere. It has some of the steepest cliffs and biggest drops. Many freeriders spend whole seasons in this amazing environment.

A typical resort has different types of terrain, so snowboarders have lots of options. Here is what most riders can find at the resort of their choice:

Piste

Pistes/Trails

Pistes, or trails, are paths that lead the skiing and snowboarding traffic around the resort. They can be narrow, wide, steep, smooth, or bumpy, but they are usually the safest way of getting around. They are cleaned each night by huge machines called snowcats.

Off-Piste

When there is fresh snow, many snowboarders love to ride the parts of a mountain that are unmarked by trails. These areas are still within the boundaries of the resort but range from tree runs to open fields of powder. They're a playground for experienced riders, but can be dangerous, as we will see later.

Backcountry

Backcountry refers to the areas of the mountain that are outside the resort boundaries. They can be the most dangerous. The backcountry is basically the mountain wilderness. It has huge appeal for many riders, but it is very dangerous due to avalanche risk and unpredictable weather. Being stuck in a remote region of the mountains in a raging blizzard can be life-threatening.

Pistes (or "trails") are ranked according to color. The easiest runs are green and blue. Red usually stands for intermediate. Black is the most difficult, and double black is for experts only!

The weather in the mountains can change very quickly. A snowboarder can be caught in harsh conditions if he or she is not careful. As a rider, the more you know about snow, the more comfortable you'll be on the mountain. Here are some facts you might not know about snow.

Temperature

People often say, "It's too cold to snow." This idea is false. As long as there is moisture in the air and a way for it to rise and form clouds, there can be snow — even in temperatures well below zero. Most heavy snowfalls occur in temperatures of 15° F (-9° C) or above, however.

Blizzards

While fresh snow is fun to ride, it can also be dangerous. If winds are greater than 35 mph (56 km/h) and visibility is at less than ¼ mile (.4 km) for more than 3 hours, heavy snowfall is considered a blizzard.

SNOWBOARDING

A rider enjoys fresh powder.

Types of Snow

Snow is different around the world. Individual snow crystals contain different amounts of liquid. For example, snow in New England may contain 4 inches (10 cm) of water for every 10 inches (25 cm) on the ground. Drier snow such as that found in the Pyrenees (Spain/France) may have less than half an inch of water (1 cm) for every 10 inches. This drier snow is favored by riders. It is called "powder." Fresh powder is any rider's dream. It is very dry, so the board glides a lot faster.

The slopes are empty as a blizzard rages.

Blizzards are extremely destructive. Riders should avoid being caught in them at all costs.

In the early days of snowboarding, it was easy to decide where to go riding, because so few resorts actually allowed it. Today, snowboarders have many choices when it comes to booking a trip.

The Atlas Mountains, Morocco

Morocco

Yes, you can go riding in Morocco, a hot country on the northwest coast of Africa. Morocco is one of the only places in the world where you can surf in great conditions one day, and then snowboard the next.

These mountains in Greenland
will challenge any rider.

Where Next?

As snowboarding becomes more popular, riders have to work at
finding less crowded slopes. Exotic places like Greenland, Russia,
and even Antarctica have been explored by riders looking for the
next best thing. With frigid temperatures and peaks of up to
16,066 feet (4897 meters), these locations are an incredible
challenge for even the most experienced pro!

The mountains of
Antarctica are the
ultimate challenge
for thrill-seeking
snowboarders.

Avalanches are terrifying forces of nature that can destroy whole towns as well as single snow slopes. An avalanche is a very large and sudden rush of snow down a mountain. Sometimes known as slides, avalanches are difficult to predict and extremely frightening. Experienced riders will sometimes turn away from a slope that looks unstable. At the very least, they ALWAYS carry the following kit:

Transceiver

Sometimes called a beeper, a transceiver is a rider's lifeline. It gives out a signal so that the buried rider can be found. This reduces the amount of time a victim is trapped by the avalanche.

SNOWBOARDING

Legends We've Lost

Even the most talented pros can succumb to the deadly power of an avalanche. In recent years, four-time world freeriding champion Craig Kelly (above) and Tommy Brunner, one of Europe's most experienced backcountry riders, have been killed by avalanches.

Probe

A probe is a folding marker that can be placed in the snow above a buried victim to pinpoint his or her location.

Shovel

A shovel is essential for digging out a victim. Pros and serious backcountry riders always carry one.

Backpack

Riders carry a backpack to store their shovel, probe, and other essentials, such as food and a first-aid kit.

No matter how experienced or well-equipped, a rider should never underestimate the power of an avalanche. Even the pros know that the best gear can't always protect them.

A house is buried by an avalanche.

How?

Settled snow is made up of many layers. A new layer forms every time it snows. Some of these layers gradually join together and form a "snow cover." Others remain separated from the layers above and below. If the layers remain separated, they can pull apart and send snow sliding down the mountain. In order to set off an avalanche, a trigger usually sets the snow sliding, such as the weight of a snowboarder or skier.

When?

The most common months for avalanches in the Northern Hemisphere are, in order: February, March, and January, due to the heavy snowfall. Although 80 percent of avalanches occur after a major snowfall, a large number also occur in periods of thaw. Most of these take place in April.

Rescuers search for an avalanche victim with a probe and shovel.

A powder avalanche tears down a slope.

Where?

Avalanches can occur on slopes with angles of as little as 25 degrees. Roughly 90 percent of all avalanches start on slopes of 30 to 45 degrees. Most skiing and snowboarding slopes are between 25 and 50 degrees.

Avalanches There are different types of avalanches. The fastest are powder avalanches, which consist of very dry snow. They can reach speeds of more than 187 mph (301 km/h).

Japanese rider Sinsuke Saitou performs an Indie grab at about 14 feet (4 meters) in the air.

For many riders, the best part of snowboarding is jumping and leaving the ground. Because snowboarding evolved from skateboarding, tricks and jumps have always been an important part of the sport.

Riders use quarter pipes to gain high air and perform elaborate tricks.

Quarter Pipe

As the name suggests, a quarter pipe is basically half of a halfpipe. Riders aim straight at the fearsome wall of the quarter pipe and are shot into the air. They then land on the same wall, creating a graceful arc in the air.

Jump A jump is a purpose-built pile of snow that riders use to get air. Today, resorts spend lots of money making sure that riders have enough jumps to keep them entertained.

Fun Parks

Designed to look like the skate parks of the 1970s and 1980s, most big resorts now have fun parks for snowboarders. These parks have handrails, a variety of imaginative jumps, and all sorts of obstacles, from picnic benches to cars.

Halfpipe

Riders use a half pipe to reach for the skies and perform complicated stunts. If you've seen the Olympics, then you know what to expect – death-defying leaps in front of huge crowds. The world's first snowboard halfpipe was shaped by skateboarder Mark Anolik near Tahoe City, California, in 1979. It became a training ground for early American freestylers such as Terry Kidwell and Keith Kimmel.

International freestyling pro Quentin Robbins

As we've seen, jibbing was developed when riders began to copy skateboarding tricks on handrails and concrete ledges. Jibbing became an underground movement that brought new fans to the sport.

Why would snowboarding, a mountain sport, look to inner city handrails for inspiration? Back in the 1980s, snowboarding was looking for its own identity. Freestyle was beginning to become popular, but many ski resorts did not allow snowboarders on their slopes. Jibbing opened up a whole new world for snowboarders to explore. They could practice their moves wherever there was fresh snow.

Pioneering freestyle snowboarder and jibber Jeremy Jones

Eighteen-year-old U.S. rider Jake Blauvelt at the Winter X Games finals (2005)

By the mid 1990s, jibbing had become less popular. By this point, many ski resorts had welcomed snowboarders. But jibbing slowly began to gain popularity again in Salt Lake City, Utah. As word began to spread, kids around the world realized that they didn't need to go to resorts to get their kicks — all they needed was a patch of snow, a handrail, and their imaginations. Companies began to make jib-specific boards, and pros could make a career doing nothing but handrails. Jibbing was back, and it was big business.

Today, jibbers practice tricks that they perform on snow or in urban areas. Some jibbers just ride rails — and rarely bother riding the rest of the resort!

Tricks

A trick is basically anything a rider does that involves leaving the ground or using an obstacle to perform a stunt. One of the coolest things about both skateboarding and snowboarding is the way the tricks are named. The person who invents the trick gets to pick the name. That means there are some odd trick names out there! For instance, some skateboarders name new tricks after their favorite food. There is a whole group of "food grabs" with names ranging from "Roast Beef" to "Chicken Salad."

British pro Adam Gendle performs an Indie grab.

Grabs

Most of the strange trick names refer to grabs. Grabs are the basis of snowboarding freestyle. Because skateboards don't have bindings, skaters learned to grab their boards to stabilize themselves in the air. By grabbing the board in different places, they could make up new tricks. Soon there were more grabs than anyone could keep track of, and snowboarders began to imitate them.

Method

One of the most challenging grabs is the Method. This is basically grabbing the heel edge of the board between your feet with your front hand, and pushing your back leg out. It is very difficult and a good measure of a rider's skill.

Indie

The easiest grab – the Indie – is just grabbing the board between your toes with your back hand. It is very natural, but it is still a very stylish trick. (See image opposite.)

Roast Beef

The Roast Beef is a classic food grab. It consists of grabbing the toe edge of the board with your back hand after putting it through your legs from the back. Sound tricky? It can be!

For most people, the death-defying stunts and spins are what make snowboarding so exciting. Since the beginning, riders have been trying to outdo each other with their toughest tricks. Spins are basically multiples of one complete (360 degrees) rotation. So a "360" means one full spin, and a "720" is two complete spins. Then it gets complicated!

One of the first skate tricks to cross over to the snow world was the McTwist. It was invented by skateboarder Mike McGill in 1985. The trick is an upside down 540-degree rotation. This means the rider completes 1½ full spins in midair before touching down on the snow again.

World freestyle champion Terje Håkonsen performs a McTwist.

A rider performs a frontside 360.

Markku Koski of Finland landed the first ever backward 1440 (four full rotations) in competition. He did it during the halfpipe competition at the U.S. Open in 2002, where he went on to take second place.

Markku Koski performs a 1440.

In 1998, when the video game "1080 Snowboarding" was introduced, actually doing a 1080 (three full rotations) on a snowboard was more of a concept than a reality. The trick is now fairly common. In 2007, German pro David Benedek was famously captured on film doing a trick called a "double-corked 1080." That's three full rotations spun like a corkscrew!

U.S. gold medalist Hannah Teter performs in the halfpipe at the 2006 Winter Olympics.

Most riders are just in it for fun, but there are a growing number of professional snowboarders. They compete in contests around the world.

Top pros battle it out in fun parks, halfpipes, and over big air jumps. They are usually judged by a panel of experts. The judges look at how well the tricks are executed, how high the riders go, and how unique the performances are. Riders around the world take part in the following contests.

Air and Style

One of snowboarding's most prestigious competitions, the Air and Style is also one of the oldest. It is held in the Olympic Stadium in Munich, Germany. The world's best freestyle riders compete on huge ramps, performing some amazing and record-breaking tricks.

Travis Rice on his way to winning the Air and Style 2006

Sponsorship at Contests

Many pros can only afford to snowboard for a living because they are sponsored. This means they get money in return for advertising for a company at contests. Top-earning U.S. pro Shaun White has sponsorship deals with many companies, including Burton and Sony Playstation. He is said to have earned $1 million in 2006. This is not typical, of course. Most pros earn around $400 per contest won.

Winter X Games

Each year, the Winter X Games take place in the United States. Athletes take part in skiing, snowboarding, snowmobiling, and snowskating competitions. The X Games often feature never before seen stunts. Competitors can win gold, silver, and bronze medals. They can also win prize money. The grand total of prize money is $1 million.

Martin Cernik from the Czech Republic performs a backside 360 at the 2002 Winter X Games.

The fact that snowboarding is now an Olympic sport is a sign that the sport is becoming more mainstream. At the 2006 Olympic Games, there were 62 competitors, whose amazing performances were watched by 30,000 spectators.

Disciplines

Today, snowboarders compete in halfpipe, parallel giant slalom (a downhill race), and snowboard cross – an exciting race between many competitors with jumps, banks, and other obstacles. Top experts judge their skill, speed, and style. Men and women compete separately.

Men's parallel giant slalom competition, 2006 Winter Olympics

SNOWBOARDING

The men's snowboard cross competition at the 2006 Winter Olympics

Snowboarding was introduced as an offical Olympic sport at the 1998 Winter Games in Nagano, Japan. Snowboarders from around the world competed in giant slalom and halfpipe events. Canada's Ross Rebliagati was the first snowboarder to win gold in the men's giant slalom event. France's Karine Ruby took home the gold for the women's giant slalom event.

Men's snowboard cross competition, 2006 Winter Olympics

When snowboarding appeared in the 1998 Olympics, the resort of Nagano (which hosted the halfpipe event) still hadn't opened its lift to regular snowboarders! It finally lifted the ban two seasons later, which is another example of how young the sport still is, and how quickly it is catching on around the world.

Ingemar's Air

Swedish snowboarder Ingemar Backman smashed the record for the world's highest quarter pipe air in 1996. He was measured at 24.6 feet (7.5 meters) high. The feat became so legendary that it is still simply known as "Ingemar's Air."

Every few years, someone comes along and breaks the height barrier.

Heikki Sorsa

Finland's Heikki Sorsa recorded the highest ever quarter pipe air when he styled an amazing Method grab over Holmenkollen Stadium in Oslo, Norway, at the 2001 Arctic Challenge. The air measured at 31.1 feet (9.5 meters) and earned him the nickname "The Flying Sorsa."

Sorsa performs his trademark Method grab.

Terje

Norwegian Terje Håkonsen added to his legendary status in March 2007 when he broke Heikki's record at the Oakley Arctic Challenge event. Terje hit an incredible 32.1 feet (9.8 meters) in height – and performed a 360 while he was at it!

Terje Håkonsen was the first rider to have a snowboarding movie made exclusively about himself. The movie, *Subjekt Haakonsen*, was released in 1996 and featured the riding of Terje and friends.

Height records are not the only way to measure snowboarding greatness. Who else has played a part in the history of snowboarding? These are some of the most astounding contributions to the development of the sport.

Amazing Jumps

In 2003, American Mike Basich made the largest drop from an aircraft on a snowboard. He jumped out of a helicopter at around 110 feet (34 meters). Mike is currently the only pro to specialize in this extreme stunt.

SNOWBOARDING

Legendary pro Terje Håkonsen recently became the first known person to ride a wave on a snowboard. He was towed into a wave by a jet ski in Hossegor, France, wearing his full snowboarding garb: boots, bindings, goggles, and pants.

Think you've been to the top of the hill? On May 24, 2001, Marco Siffredi became the first person to climb and ride down Mount Everest. Marco rode from the summit to Advanced Base Camp, recording a total vertical drop of 8,032 feet (2,448 meters)! On a second attempt to ride down the steeper north face of the mountain in 2002, Marco disappeared. He was never seen again.

The North Face, Mount Everest

Need for Speed

The fastest snowboarder in the world is Australia's Darren Powell. He rode his board at an eye-wateringly scary 125.459 mph (201.907 km/h) at the "Flying Kilometer" championships in France on May 2, 1999. The seven-time world speed snowboard champ wears gear that is designed to be extremely aerodynamic, including a streamlined helmet.

Who are snowboarding's most influential riders? As you might imagine, this is something that fans have endlessly debated over the years. As in any sport, some people have more of an impact than others. Here are some of the true greats:

Jake Burton Carpenter

In 1977, Jake Burton Carpenter started Burton Snowboards from a workshop on his farm in Vermont. Today, it is estimated that half the snowboards sold in the world have his name on them. And he still rides 100 days a year!

Shaun White

Nicknamed "The Flying Tomato" because of his red hair, Shaun White rose to fame as one of the youngest snowboarding pros. He gained sponsorship from the snowboarding manufacturer Burton when he was only 6 years old! He has gone on to win a gold medal in at least one international championship each year since 2003, including the Winter Olympic Games in 2006.

Craig Kelly

U.S. pro Craig Kelly was the first freeriding professional. He quit the contest scene to ride powder and is referred to as the "Godfather of Freeriding." He was sadly killed in 2003, but his influence looms large.

Terje Håkonsen

Without a doubt, Terje Håkonsen is a legendary snowboarder. The quiet Norwegian has won every type of contest and has also made some of the best films. He topped a 2004 poll as the most influential snowboarder on the planet. His name has been loaned to two snowboard tricks: the Håkonflip and the J-Tear, which is his first name partially reversed.

Hannah Teter

The 2006 Olympic gold winner Hannah Teter is a master of the halfpipe. Born in Vermont, Hannah became the first woman to land a 900 in a halfpipe competition at age 15.

Tom Sims

This snowboarding pioneer from New Jersey was an accomplished skateboarder. In 1963, Tom Sims attempted to re-create the feeling of skating on snow by sliding down a hill on a board he had built as a high school project. In 1977, he started producing snowboards in his garage under the Sims name.

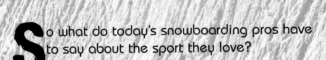

So what do today's snowboarding pros have to say about the sport they love?

> **"** I can't believe how hard the first couple of days snowboarding were in the very beginning. I don't think anyone really gets a break from those, no matter how talented they turn out to be! ... That's one thing which is really great about snowboarding: the fun and challenge of progressing never stop. **"**

David Benedek, Germany

"I've had some really scary situations in Alaska ... we were hiking along the ridge with cornices on either side. It's really dangerous. The guy was about four meters in front of me, and I said, 'On the left here, there's a cornice' and as he took one step to the side, the whole cornice just went ... I think that was about as scared as I've been. I've been in one avalanche. It was scary because it happened so quick. I got to a tree as well, and I felt pretty confident holding that tree. That was in Mount Baker, about 15 years ago."

Terje Håkonsen, Norway

"Snowboarding is fun to me because you get to travel all the time ... which I think is why I still do it so much. I've been to places that I never would have been to without snowboarding, and I always go with my friends. There's also something extra special about doing an activity that's in nature. You get so exhilarated by just being in the mountains that it makes snowboarding even better."

Adam Gendle, United Kingdom

Glossary

Aerodynamic Having a shape that reduces the air drag and therefore enhances speed

Air The amount of time a rider spends off the ground

Cornice An overhanging mass of snow or ice, usually on a ridge

Frontside and Backside This refers to which the way the spin goes — left or right. If the rider spins so that the front of her body faces outward, it is called a frontside spin. If she spins so her back faces outward, it is a backside spin.

Monoski An inspiration for the snowboard. The rider stands on the middle of the board with his feet together facing forward, and wiggles his hips to turn.

Nose and Tail The front (nose) and back (tail) of a snowboard, relating to the direction the rider travels in

Powder Deep, fluffy snow that most snowboarders prefer

Shredding A slang term for snowboarding

Skate Park Concrete and wooden parks for skateboarding that becaome popular in the 1970s. Snowboarders copied the idea at resorts, and called them fun parks.

Skateboarding A hugely popular urban sport that in many ways provides snowboarding with its roots and culture

Snow Cover The layers of snow that fall over the course of the winter, and settle to make one thick layer. Also called a "snow pack."

Snowboard Cross An exciting race (sometimes called boardercross) between a group of snowboarders over a course with jumps, steep corners, and other obstacles

Spins Most snowboarding tricks are based on spin. Some experienced boarders can spin 360 degrees or more in the air.

Streamlined Offering very little wind resistance

Surfing The original board sport, from which skateboarding and snowboarding originated

Thaw The thaw comes when the snow melts as spring arrives

Toe Edge/Heel Edge The edges of a snowboard bordering on the heels or toes of the rider

Wax Snowboarders apply wax to the base of their board to make sure it glides smoothly on the snow. It is melted onto the base using an iron and then scraped off for a smooth finish.

Index

About the Author

Matt Barr is a snowboarder and journalist from Manchester,
England. He has traveled across the world, visiting places like
Lebanon and Russia. Matt has written for many snowboarding
publications, including *Whitelines* magazine.